A Schizophrenic, A Bomber
and A Woodworker
Walk Into a Bar

DEDICATION

For My Son Jason
1970-2013

Jason, I think of you often.

I wish I had been better
at knowing how smart you were.

A Schizophrenic, A Bomber
and A Woodworker Walk Into a Bar

Memoir of a Survivor

By Randy Estabrook

Editor
Sandra Olivetti Martin
New Bay Books
Fairhaven, Maryland
NewBayBooks@gmail.com

Cover and interior design by Suzanne Shelden
Shelden Studios
Prince Frederick, Maryland
sheldenstudios@comcast.net

A Note on Type:
Cover and section heads and text
are set in Gatlin Bold WF.
Body text is set in Garamond Premier Pro.

Library of Congress
Cataloging-in-Publication Data

ISBN 979-8-9882998-4-4

Printed in the United States of America
First Edition

TABLE OF CONTENTS

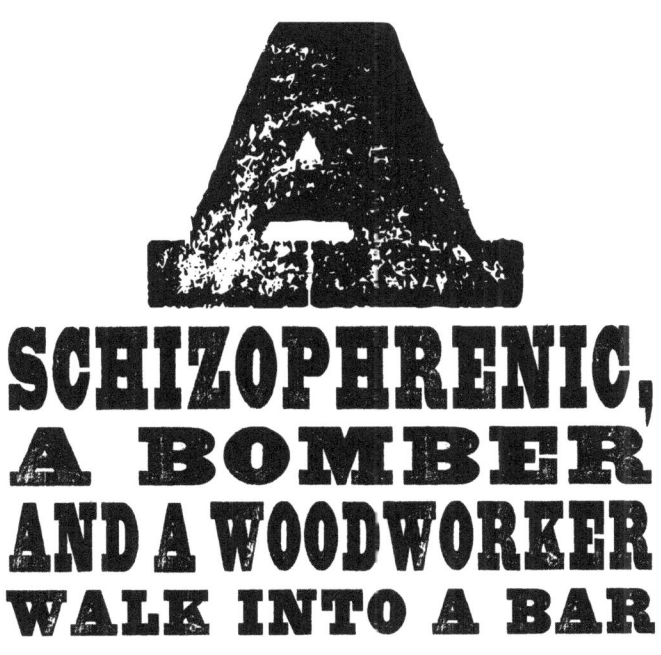

A SCHIZOPHRENIC, A BOMBER AND A WOODWORKER WALK INTO A BAR

Memoir of a Survivor

By Randy Estabrook

THE NOTORIOUS MILLER TWINS

"What's your earliest memory?" Dr. Terry asks. "I mean when you think back, how old were you and what were you doing?"

"I was about three, I think, standing up on the milk delivery box on the front porch trying to reach into the mailbox and retrieve something," I offer.

"That's pretty good, three years old, you're pretty sure about that?"

"I don't know why that popped into my head, but I'm gonna go with it."

"What else pops into your head?" Dr. Terry says.

There was more than meets the eye to Dr. Terry's question. Sigmund Freud had taught analysts to look deeper. The earliest memory was a screen, he believed, for hotter issues that lay hidden beneath blander, more benign events. The father of psychoanalysis was not far off in my case.

"I remember coming and getting in bed with my mother early in the mornings. There was touching and fondling, but not in a violent manner," I say, surprising myself.

"I'm not sure this is accurate, maybe I'm making this up, I'm not sure this actually happened."

"Well, you're the one making it up," Dr. Terry says.

"I remember early mornings crawling in bed with my mother, it was intimate and special. Caressing, touching and lots of hugs, her fondling my little thing. I know that a mother and child have a special bond, but this was outside those lines, I mean my father was asleep right next to us. Crazy, right?"

Over days, weeks, months of digging with Dr. Terry, my memories filled out.

I was an unruly brat, a real pain-in-the-ass kid, but hey, with all this shit going on maybe it was justified.

Like the time I got my sister to get in the dryer, then turned it on, just for a moment. When I got in trouble, my mother took me to the basement, telling me to get a stick from the kindling box. "Bring it to me" she said. "Turn around and pull your pants down," she ordered.

Crying uncontrollably, I pulled my pants down slowly, mortified and private about my body like most kids of that age.

Then she started hitting me with the stick.

After what seemed like years, on one visit to the basement when I was told to go get the stick, I hesitated.

"What's wrong? Go get the stick." She said it like it was somehow amusing.

I said, "we're not doing this anymore." I think I was nine years old.

Until I saw Dr. Terry, all this trauma was pretty much hidden behind all the mostly normal memories of growing up.

What had brought me to Dr. Terry was my impotence in my relationship with Patricia, who would become my second wife in 1985. I thought there was something wrong with me. If Dr. Terry thought this process would help me, I was willing to try.

I spent 12 years sorting things out, and yes, it did help. Moving through time, here's what I discovered.

THE ESTABROOK FAMILY: 1960S

We lived in a nice suburban Bethesda home and belonged to the county club. I sang in the church choir, and Dad was an attorney. Mom was a talented portrait painter, member of the garden club and volunteered. Normal, right?

Here's what normal was like at 5609 Springfield Drive, Bethesda, Maryland.

One morning, I was heading out the door to school when my mother said, "Your father has the phones bugged. He's listening to everything we say. Did you know that?"

"Uh, no, I was not aware," I said. "I have to go."

Where did this shit come from?

I mean, my father coming home night after night, wrestling with the dog, then taking up his post behind the *Evening Star* while my mother would hurl accusations, innuendo and outright insults from the kitchen.

"I know you are having me followed," she harangued, as my father turned the page. "The phone is bugged. Why are you doing this?" "I know you are making a lot more money than you are telling me," she railed. "And then there is the affair," she said in retreat.

This whole exchange, without even as much as a reply, so angered me. Wasn't anyone going to stand up to this?

Apparently not. When I challenged my mother, my father defended her.

Once, he confronted me. My accusations had became heated. "What's wrong with you? Why do you put up with this crap over and over?" I demanded.

We argued, and he grabbed me and spanked me. "Go to your room," he yelled. I must have been nine or ten.

Years later, when I was in my 30s and he was in his 70s, he talked about what he couldn't do then, giving me a family history. I wish I had known this much earlier. It might have saved a few therapy dollars.

He said early on he would respond, defend himself against the seemingly unhinged attacks, but slowly he realized it was fruitless. Silence seemed to be best.

He said it was not uncommon for him and my mother to go out to a restaurant and get halfway through the meal when my mother would excuse herself from the table. She would not return.

"I would wait, when it started, for a half hour or more," he said. "I would ask someone to check the ladies' room to see if she was inside," he added. "She wasn't. Then I realized she had left and gone home."

"On later occasions I waited a shorter amount of time before realizing she wasn't coming back," he concluded.

Kathleen Miller was an attractive woman. I imagine most of us feel this way when we look at old photos of our parents, but I grew up thinking my mother was pretty. She was young, and she looked happy. Often acted happy, too. But as I go through family photos I can see her facial expressions change, an eerie suggestion that she is going through some sort of transformation.

In the early days, when she was still herself, parties were frequent, as often as every weekend. They had bridge parties, cocktail parties, even dinner parties. I remember their good friends the Coombs were a regular jovial fixture on the weekend.

Before the guests arrived, my sisters and I would usually be relegated to our bedrooms, either by direct order or a strong suggestion. Tracy, eight years older, must have already been off on her own, for she remembers none of this.

Carol, Laurie and I would take turns sneaking down the stairs, peering around the corner to take in all the festivities, punctuated by ice clinking in glasses and roaring laughter. It was festive, it was exciting. Then it seemed, without warning, it stopped.

My clearest memory that our family life was breaking down comes at Christmas, when my sisters and I—all of us young kids—were so excited. Confident that Santa had stopped by, we got up early.

Our home was a early mid-century split level with the lower level being the den. Until my parents rose on Christmas morning, the door to the downstairs den was locked with a knitted Santa face tied around the knob for extra Christmas emphasis. There was no sneaking in to peek at what was beyond. Our imaginations were out of control. Was there a new 10-speed bike? New winter clothes, the latest games—well, you all know the drill.

Far later than we kids wanted, my parents would get up, probably after a long night setting everything up, and we would have the ceremonial opening of the Christmas cavern. It was exciting and very much a normal (that word again) family Christmas, complete with dazzlingly wrapped packages, colorful stockings brimming with candy, treats and surprises. It would commence with the opening of packages and the related screams of joy and delight.

Then almost without warning, as if a switch was thrown, my mother would start to dim like a set of headlights. It was a progressive decline.

Before long the transformation became uncomfortable, scary, even alarming like *what is happening to our mother in real time?* The scene would degrade to the point of shouts, argument and an almost planned retreat my mother would make to her bedroom upstairs.

My father and older sisters would rally, all of us moving to the kitchen for French toast, bacon and orange juice—saved by the goodness of food.

LOOKING BACK: THE MILLER FAMILY

Where did this shit come from?

To try to understand, I look back half a century and more to my mother's early life—or as close as I can get to it through my early memories of her family.

The life my seemingly carefree young parents lived was a cut above my mother's childhood. She grew up in northeast Washington, D.C., she and her identical, and I mean identical, twin beginning a family of six kids. The lone brother was named Alan. Her father, Fred, worked for the Pennsylvania and Ohio Railroad.

My father's family grew up on the other side of D.C., in northwest Washington, and later over the D.C. line in Chevy Chase, Maryland.

Chevy Chase was an enclave not accessible by many. Tied for the most affluent town in America, it has two separate country clubs. It boasts being the most educated town in America with 93 percent of residents having at least a bachelor degree. My father, an attorney, had two degrees. So in becoming Mrs. Estabrook, my mother married up.

Our family's prosperity gave at least one of her sisters, Virginia, more reason to resent my mother. Though she was years younger than the twins—the baby before Shirley came along—she felt the twins had stolen her childhood.

"Everybody doted on them," she said.

Then my mother married well, while Virginia, always called Chub—which I'm sure was short for Chubby, for it was accurate—married Uncle Jack, who was a fan, actually a big fan, of the drink, as they say in some countries.

Chub didn't like my father, either. I can remember her taunts: "How is Willie?" she would ask, choosing a nickname that she knew would get my goat.

"His name is William, and he's good," I responded through clenched teeth.

"I don't know why, but I think of him as Willie, always in a suit and so proper," she said.

Despite the tension, I remember spending the night at Chub's apartment with my cousins Ressa Ann and Rex. I can remember after us kids had gone to bed, the loud conversations between Jack and Chub, who was a drinker in her own right. Jack, who was intermittently in residence, would get home late, and the fireworks would start.

Chub and Jack lived just around the corner from my grandfather, Fred, a tall and slender man with a crew cut and a couple of tattoos, one on each forearm. Some folks would call them railroad tattoos, and they'd be pretty accurate in that description. Fred worked for the Pennsylvania and Ohio railroad for 40 years. I asked more than once to see what I thought was the legendary retirement watch, but it never materialized.

Fred was married to Frederica, right? I know: not in a million years. Frederica was a force not to be reckoned with. She was maybe five feet tall and five feet wide, but she did not tolerate any back talk from anyone, including Fred. She was the originator of the Miller family Hoe cake, a delicious form of thick flat bread with sugar and cinnamon and of course, butter.

We would visit often it seemed before Frederica passed away.

Fred and Chub were, if not the founders, certainly the most vigilant supporters of the Friday Night Club. Fred would hang a silk banner above the entry to the kitchen that said, The Friday Night Club, and the bar was open. I think some friend sent the silk banner to Fred from Japan.

Fred would get a bit liquored up and want to wrestle, mostly me. It was supposed to be in fun, but I didn't think so.

I had much less interaction with the rest of my mother's family.

An early summer or two, I stayed at Great Aunt Cornelius' (we called her Aunt Corney) farm and had a fine time—except when the oldest Miller child, Alan, was around. He was a prickly farmer that I didn't much like, but his wife was possibly the nicest person I can remember. With Aunt Shirley, I felt safe and protected, maybe from Alan.

Jane, the next oldest sister, was married to Henry, an ophthalmologist who worked at National Institutes of Health. I remember visiting their home in Georgetown and being impressed that they lived in the city. Jane seemed stuck up, while Henry, an avid sailor, spoke of it frequently. Chub probably resented them, too.

Shirley, the last sister, was even more distant. She was married to Fritz, who had taught at the Citadel, so they lived in South Carolina with their five sons. Fritz was an odd one, and domineering. When Fredericka visited her youngest daughter, family legend has it, she brought along her own toilet paper. "I'm not having anybody tell me how many sheets I can use," she said.

The last time I saw Fritz, at a sister's funeral, he handed me a business card that said Ships in Bottles, Langley, Virginia.

I said, "What's this about?"

He responded, "It's lengthy, I could tell you, but then I'd have to kill you."

"CIA? What a sweetheart," I said.

Pauline was unaccountably distant from my childhood family life. Unaccountably because, first, she was mother's twin. Second, her husband Stan, had attended law school with my father at night, possibly when they both returned from World War II. He'd dropped out and become a dentist, so the Hagens were well off. They lived less than a mile from us but were not in the same social circles; the two families' kids went to different schools.

What kept the twins apart at this stage in their lives I can't say. The only clue might have been Stan's alcoholism, which later killed him.

Pauline worked as a legal secretary, and I imagine after Stan passed away it was not easy caring for three children—my cousins Cathy, Steve and Jamie on just her salary. She always seemed upbeat and cheery and never remarried and as far as I know she didn't have any other relationships, she just toughed it out. I remember that my father, who had good luck financially, helped her out.

Despite the distance my mother and Pauline kept from one another, Cathy, Steve and Jamie were my closest cousins. So in my review, I include them, too.

Holiday get-togethers and periodic dinners brought us together, usually at Pauline's house.

I idolized my older cousins Steve and Jaimie, who seemed so bohemian and cool, beyond the stiff private-school structure that I lived in at the time. They had their bedrooms in the basement and seemed to live an unsupervised life. Nobody was messing with them. I was jealous.

Steve and Jaimie's sister Cathy was closer to my age and as younger kids, would come over to play with me and Laurie, my younger sister. We got along well. But over the years, we went our separate ways.

She'd moved to San Francisco and step by step was running very successful restaurants in South Park. Her success impressed me. I'd achieved some success myself, with Apple, my furniture and woodworking company's most valuable account.

When I visited Apple and invited a few of my clients to my cousin's restaurant, South Park Cafe, they were impressed with my connection, for Cathy's restaurants were some of the late 1980s' hottest.

Dinner was amazing, the cuisine was French and Cathy visited our table and talked about the challenges of running a restaurant and of the areas requiring the most focus: One was remembering every patron's name so that they would feel special and return.

After dinner the conversation turned to Cathy's and my childhoods, and she started sharing memories.

They were starkly different than mine. "You guys were so privileged," she started. "I mean the country club membership, we never had that! The cotillion, private schools, vacations, you were so privileged!" she snapped.

I felt the floor open up and was praying that I would somehow disappear through it. I looked around the table and noticed the look of shock on my clients' faces. All I could think was "You've kept this bottled up for how long?"

What I thought would be a nice dinner and a family bonding event couldn't have been more different. The resentments of my parents' generation had spilled over into mine. Who I was now made no difference to her; all she could see of me was the boy she envied a quarter century earlier.

Over the years, I also re-encountered my boy cousins.

Jaimie had enlisted in the army and gone to Vietnam. I bumped into him one day at the Drug Fair on Westbard Avenue, my old hangout in junior high school, after he had returned from duty.

In my eyes, he was doubly a man, in age and in experience. "I have trouble with girls, don't know how to talk to them," I confided to him, feeling safe because he was, after all, my cousin—my mother's twin sister's son.

"You need to keep your eyes above their chest, on their eyes and stay focused," he said.

Our conversation moved on to his life in the army. "What was it like?" I asked.

"It was not the greatest experience," he said. "We were on the front lines and doing enemy recon; it was scary stuff. I remember one night that forever changed my life. We were on a night recon mission when I saw movement out of the corner of my left eye. I turned and fired. I went over to investigate, and my world changed forever. It was a woman and her two children. I cannot erase it."

Still in my mid teens, not much younger than Jamie had been when he went to Vietnam, I couldn't imagine the kind of horror he was talking about. I'd wanted to feel close to him, connected, but this was too close for comfort.

Jamie never recovered. He overdosed on the same drugs he had learned to use over there.

Steve seemed the normal one in the Hagen family when we reconnected years later. He was living in Olney, Maryland, with a woman and her children and had a bit of a farm that they worked hard on, with a multitude of vegetables to show for it.

Steve's day job was in concrete construction, foundations mostly, and I asked him "What's with the rigid posture?" He lifted the back of his shirt and turned around. "Had some work done on a few vertebrae," he said. I looked in shock at the scars. "This is what carrying two five-gallon buckets of concrete up the steps to pour the hearth does to you," he said.

He seemed uninjured in mind, however, both strong and optimistic.

Much later, when Cathy was in town for a family funeral, she told me Steve's secret: He had continued his brother's correspondence from Vietnam, writing to himself as if he were Jamie.

Wherever my family's shit came from, it was all around me.

RECONCILIATION

I married early, at 18, after my girlfriend admitted she'd forgotten to take her birth control pills. We lived in Gaithersburg, I found a job in a cabinet shop and had three children by the time I was 25. So my mother no longer held sway over my life.

After my parents' divorce, she moved to Woodstock, Virginia, where her mother grew up.

Woodstock is a charming small Virginia town, the county seat of Shenandoah County, nestled in the seven bends of the Shenandoah River. The town itself is 3.2 square miles and surrounded by farms, livestock and pastures.

There, oddly, she bought the very house Frederica was born in.

With 100 miles between us, I thought she couldn't touch me.

When my second son Ryan was born, I called my mother to tell her.

"Oh, that's wonderful," she said. "What did you name him?"

"Ryan Douglas," I responded.

"Why Randy, that's a Catholic name," she said.

I hung up.

I kept my distance until I got a phone call from my mother's sister Jane. She pulled me right back into it.

"You know, Randy, your mother is living in a house with no heat or water," Jane said.

"Wow," I said. "What do you expect me to do?"

"I don't know," she said. "I just thought you should know."

I was furious, at Jane, at my mother, at what this would mean for me. I couldn't do nothing, even though I wanted to, so off I went. This was during the gas crisis in the 1970s. I would fill up a five-gallon jerrican so I could make the trip. My Chevy Vega station wagon would not make the round trip on one tank. But gas turned out to be more plentiful in Woodstock.

The house was an older framed construction farmhouse with the basic peaked-style roof and a white picket fence surrounding it on its corner lot.

Frederica's parents' old farmhouse was a little rundown outside; inside it was worse. Jane was right: no heat, no running water. My mother had started to refinish some of the woodwork. But she had not gotten the fuel oil tank refilled, so the furnace stopped and the water pipes froze. The fire department had had to turn off the water after the basement filled up and spilled down the street. It took them a day to pump out the dirt floor basement.

My mother lived with a space heater in one of the bedrooms and visited the bathroom at the courthouse to fill up water jugs to take home.

Summer was much easier.

Fixing up my mother's home became a mission. I replaced the furnace (gas was cheaper), fixed the water pipes, insulated the attic. It took months and many trips, but finally it was habitable again.

Once again it was a nice house, with plaster walls, solid wood trim, tongue-and-groove ceilings, a brick fireplace and with what I thought was a very nice staircase. One aspect I always liked but made me a bit uncomfortable was the coffin window. This was a window with an extra bottom sash to make the transport of a coffin in and out of the home possible.

With my mother's house in order, I thought things were stable enough to take my children to see their grandmother. I was wrong.

"Whose children are these? Did you rent them?" my mother asked.

"No, these are your grandchildren."

"I don't think so," she spat.

I think this was perhaps the hardest visit I made. I never brought them again.

All the time working on my mother's house, making multiple trips, enlisting friends to help, I was worried she had no money.

As it turned out, she wasn't so bad off. Her divorce settlement was in the bank. As a well-known resident of the town, she would walk into the bank and say, "I need some money," and they would give it to her so she would behave and go away.

Woodstock became her safe haven. Over the years, I became good friends with the commonwealth's attorney, Billy Logan. He was a godsend as her oddities became more extreme, and his patient phone calls to me were frequent.

The phone would ring. "Randy, your mom apparently took a bus to a boys' school in Roanoke to apply for a job. I've made arrangements to get her on a bus back to Woodstock, but I wanted you to know."

"Wow, Billy, thank you so much for taking care of that, I am in your debt," I said.

One phone call was longer. "Randy, your mom took a bus to New York City for New Year's and was mugged. Her purse and money were taken, and she has been staying in a shelter. She's okay, and I have made arrangements to put her on a bus, but it's going to D.C. Can you meet her and give her a ride back to Woodstock?"

I was thinking holy shit, wtf was she doing in New York City? What I said was, "Sure Billy, I can meet her and bring her home." That was a long ride.

Her behavior seemed to confirm the diagnosis from Western State Hospital in Staunton that my mother showed symptoms of paranoid schizophrenia, treatable with medication. However, the physician said that Kathleen felt she was fine. It was everyone else who had problems.

With that diagnosis, my sister Carol and I went in front of the local judge for a guardianship hearing. Billy was there to help, for even though he was the commonwealth attorney, he also had his own practice.

"These are not my children, Judge," Kathleen said. "I don't know who these people are, and whatever they have told you is not true," she added.

Not my children. Carol and I both flinched. This was so bizarre and hurtful.

As the judge asked Kathleen about her life, her family and her recent travels, she slowly convinced him she was a danger to herself and others.

With that decision, Carol and I were granted guardianship of our mother. She was outraged. It was maybe after that my mother started calling me Johnny Josephson. She never called me by my real name again. Carol, however, remained Carol.

Carol and I joined forces, visiting regularly to check on our mother.

By that time, the twins had reunited, Pauline joining Kathleen in Woodstock. Pauline knew who I was. "Hi Randy, how are you? Hi Carol," Pauline said when we had bumped into one another in the street one day, the approaching twins two figures bobbing almost in opposition. Kathleen, out front, called, "Hi Johnny. Hi Carol."

Despite her altered reality, Mother was an able gardener. She designed the sizeable back yard of her double lot to replicate a Williamsburg garden: It was quite impressive, with planted sections radiating out of a central circle, similar to a labyrinth. She dug it all out herself, with a shovel. But she left it unattended for a number of years, and it became so overgrown that people in town complained. We set out to clean it up and restore some order.

"I think this shed and workshop are ready to fall down," Carol said. We didn't have the resources to repair it. So, as Carol said, "How are we going to get mother to let us take it down before it falls on her?"

As we considered, I remembered my mother describing the history of the house she was living in, how it had been originally built on the banks of the Rappahannock River. I thought we could use that.

Carol and I put together a plan.

Later that day, when I had asked my mother to come outside, I turned the conversation to the shed and workshop and how it needed to be fixed up. "We are planning to disassemble these structures and return them to their original site on the banks of the Rappahannock River, to be reassembled under the guidance of the Rappahannock Historical Society."

My mother paused and gave me a long hard puzzled look, then finally said *okay* and walked away.

On another visit, she revealed that she heard voices.

"What kind of voices?" I asked.

"Our old dentist, Dr. Abro, put in a brain picker and it has been talking to me since," she said. "Like right now it's telling me not to believe anything you say."

Startled, I continued to press about the voices and what else they might be saying. "The voice is telling me not to answer you," she replied.

She also thought her car had been tampered with. She'd call the police routinely, complaining that the engine in her car was not the original engine. "Someone has replaced it with another engine," she would say. Other times, the tires had been switched.

Time after time, an officer of the small police force would visit. The officer may have thought she was just lonely and would endure the conversation and the visit.

This theme would occur over and over, the car, the plumbing pipes, the furnace, etc. In my mother's opinion, life was an evolving conspiracy of manipulation and sinister acts.

Pauline was soon adding her own stories. She offered up the new perspective that a local storage facility in Woodstock had allowed or instigated the swapping of her furniture.

"This is not the same furniture," she said. "Someone has switched it with some other furniture."

Another time, Pauline called me out of the blue. "I think there is a man living in your mother's house," she said.

"Why would you think that?" I asked.

"Well, just last night someone broke my finger while I was asleep," she offered.

"Did you wake up?" I inquired.

"Well, no," she said.

I was puzzled. How is this possible?

"You know, if someone broke my finger while I was asleep, I'm pretty sure I would wake up." I said. The conversation didn't last much longer.

Their shared delusions hit me like a punch to the gut. I couldn't catch my breath. I was dizzy with the sudden realization that they truly were identical twins, even in their paranoid schizophrenia.

Together, their trips became more ambitious. More than once, they flew to London. Arriving at Heathrow, they requested an audience with Queen Elizabeth. "We are both direct descendants," my mother would say.

They were escorted to the first flight returning to the U.S. On subsequent trips they wised up and only bought one-way tickets. The British authorities had to pay to send them back.

As the years went by, the stories accumulated.

My mother would frequent the best restaurant in town, the Spring House. It was long a fixture in Woodstock, for the food was quite good. On a good day, my mother would arrive for lunch. She was a very slow eater, but she had no schedule. After lunch she would settle the tab and move to another table. Once situated, she would order dinner.

In her remaining days, my mother developed health issues. In one last ditch effort to break through the wall and help my mother acknowledge me as her son, I wheeled Kathleen down the hill to the end of town to see a clinical therapist.

I suppose it was a selfish pursuit; I wanted the therapist's help for myself.

"Well, Randy," the therapist said, "the very fact that she is sitting here with you is in itself acknowledgement that you are her son."

I broke down in tears, sobbing uncontrollably.

THS CHARGED IN THRILL BOMBINGS —
ged by police with taking part in thrill bombings
Chevy Chase suburban area on the outskirts of
own at police headquarters after their arrest.

THE BETHESDA BOMBER

Looking both ways, I stepped out of Empire Music and locked the door. I had slipped a .38 into my pants earlier and gathered up the day's cash, ready to head to the bank night deposit drawer to relieve myself of over $2,000.

The .38 was one my father had brought home from the war. I had stumbled across it rummaging through his trunks from the Navy and felt much safer with it in these circumstances.

Empire Music was located on a less-than-ideal section of Georgia Avenue, just over the District line in Montgomery County, Maryland. On any given day, queued up outside was a parade of people who relied on public transportation as well as those unemployed and struggling to make it to tomorrow, some with all their possessions attached, some with hardly any.

It constantly amazed me that people actually came to this store to buy records. Its interior reflected the drab, well-worn, peeling paint of the neighborhood. Nothing was newer than 50 years before.

I mean there were four other much more friendly looking Empire stores with newer interiors, new record bins, carpet and ceiling tiles. The Silver Spring Store was on its last legs, drab gray walls, the oldest record bins in the chain and a curtain that separated the front room from the back. Made me feel as if the mummy would suddenly appear from behind the curtain.

The curtain split the large store in two almost equal sections. In the front, most business regarding records and tapes took place. The back was quite different. Legend has it that in prior years the soda machine was somewhat magical. You would stop at the front desk, make a contribution, and be instructed as to which type of soda you should select. You then dropped in your 25 cents to complete the transaction, but the resulting delivery was far and away from Coca-Cola or 7-Up. The delivered product was regulated by the Bureau of Narcotics and Dangerous Drugs, but was in most cases used like tobacco.

Given the history of the store's owner, about which you are soon to learn, and the periodic visits from the FBI to the Bethesda mother store, this sideline offering of a former manager was discontinued after being discovered by the owners. During my tenure, many folks lamented management's change of heart.

THE $1.99 SALE

We were the cut-price location of the chain, the perfect fit for the sometimes more-than-annual $1.99 sale. Any record you wanted for just $1.99. Hard to believe? You bet. Most records retailed for $3.99. How in the world could Jim Seward, the owner, sell a $3.99 record for $1.99?

The brilliance resided in the fact that many of the discount offerings had come from less-than-legal sources.

The process was not complicated. Entrepreneurs, who in most cases wore long raincoats in muted colors, would visit a competing store and, through the practice of slight-of-hand, would fan an entire bin of record albums under their raincoats. Somehow, miraculously, they would retain the albums and exit the store undetected. My boss, Jim, was very accepting of this unique buying opportunity, offering 10 cents on the dollar, which was, in most cases, enthusiastically accepted.

With the acquired merchandise came with the challenge of the competitors' labeling. But with practiced repackaging techniques, there was still room for an acceptable mark up of 300 percent, not a bad margin.

Harold, an underaged employee, had developed the practiced art of sealing the new clear wrappers for the albums, a tedious task as it required expert knowledge of how long to apply the mini heat iron on the material to achieve a seal. I can still smell the hot plastic, similar to when an iron is left on fabric too long only with the, I'm sure, totally safe, chemical addition, as we all breathed in some toxicity we did not know enough about.

Our $1.99 sale was a sight to see and a challenge to facilitate. The navigation dividers that typically pointed you to a particular artist or genre of music had been removed, so you were forced to wade through bin after bin of records searching for something you were looking for. This accomplished many things, among them, increasing the number of people in the store and moving inventory out the door, all good for sales.

Periodically during the day, the doors would be closed for a few minutes as the bins were salted with the prizes most were after. The sounds of discovery would periodically rise above the din, sounding like a child's giggle, as a copy of *Led Zeppelin II* came into possession. Of course, some grumbled as they completed the purchase of 10 records, about the one or two they could not find. Still they left happily, having saved $30 or more.

We at the store were happy, too, for in a day we had brought in more than an average week's sales. That's why I armed myself for these special nightly deposits. Safety, and being a big shot.

ENTERING THE EMPIRE

My guide to Empire Music was Ron Arck.

Ron and I had met in the Quad at Walt Whitman High School, an outside courtyard surrounded by the expanse of the wrapped-around school. Ron, a couple years older, was about 6 feet tall with piercing eyes. He wore his black hair long and straight. His usual outfit included a vest, denim jeans and boots. He had a calm presence, and I was quickly drawn to what seemed confidence in who he was. To this day, I imagine Ron strutting back and forth and lip-syncing the Stones' "Sympathy for The Devil." He was iconic in a Jaggeresque way. More than likely we started a discussion on the Vietnam war, local bands or the dysfunctionality of high school.

My favorite week in high school was a week titled EFFE, Experiment in Free Form Education. The format, pretty straight forward, was similar to ordering dinner at a Chinese restaurant, one from column A, B etc. From a list of subject topics and a time slot, you picked what was interesting and worked out a schedule of your selections. At the end of the week of abstract painting, I was awash in disappointment at now having to return to the drudgery of my previous boring classes.

There was the possible exception of Mrs. Pinson's class in algebra. I remember the day Mrs. Pinson noticed some students whose faces displayed an empty wandering look. Not sure of what they might be under the influence of, Mrs. Pinson made the decision to turn off the lights and gather everyone onto the class room floor for a session in meditation.

"I want you all to put away your books. We are going to try something a bit different," she said. The process included class exercises in breathing and awareness plus individual attention. "Imagine you are in a six-sided glass box," she began, "beyond which is nothingness. I want you to start by erasing the ceiling, beyond which is nothingness." Her voice was calm, confident and soothing.

This did not seem too difficult.

"I want you to stay focused on your breathing. Now I want you to erase the back wall, beyond which is nothingness."

Again, not too difficult.

Two more steps followed, until we were sitting on the last surface of the box. The next step was so uncomfortable that I opened my eyes Erasing the floor I was sitting on was, I suppose, too much loss of control.

Ron's confidence balanced my hidden anxiety. He and I became fast friends. We spent many days skipping school, riding in his Oldsmobile Cutlass convertible with his girlfriend Marty. I felt free, alive, untethered and full of adventure.

We would drive in and out of the city, but a popular destination was off Carderock Parkway on the banks of the Potomac River just above the Chesapeake and Ohio Canal. We spent countless hours climbing on rocks, admiring the calming effects of the river and engaging in those esoteric conversations about why the world was such a mess and how we could change it, a rite of passage for every 16 year old. The sound was therapeutic, the rushing falls of the river, the undulations of the scene coupled with, on a great day, sunshine. It was our oasis. I think the thing I most loved was the weekday deserted nature of this place. Any given weekend was much different, with a mostly full parking lot and hordes of hikers, bike riders and kayakers.

Weekdays, it was ours alone.

As Ron's and my friendship evolved, he talked endlessly about his job at Empire Music in Bethesda. I was fascinated. The owner, Jim Seward, sounded like such a character, a cross between hoodlum entrepreneur and musical purveyor.

One day while we were skipping school, Ron said he needed to get to work at the record store on his work-study job. He invited me along. I was all in for the new adventure.

Parking the car in the Woodmont parking garage—which later would have been renowned as the napping spot for Montgomery County's finest had not Jim resisted the temptation of documenting it on film—we walked around the corner into the 2,500-square-foot store. The front window had this large rainbow-colored sign with 4-inch thick letters in a Roman arch configuration reading Empire Music. It was hard to miss.

The front room was loaded with record bin after bin as well as wall displays of the latest albums and posters of the favorite stars of the day: Hendrix, the Stones, Johnny Winter, the Beatles, Steppenwolf and many more. I was in heaven. The sound that echoed through the store and over the music playing was unmistakable:

pinball machines. The sales counter backed up to the front window, and as soon as Ron walked behind the counter, he seemed to belong there.

Ron immediately turned up the stereo, which blared throughout the store, and began to sing, "Please allow me to introduce myself, I'm a man of wealth and taste." He seemed to be transformed into Jagger himself, the shake of the head, the sweep of the hair, the raised statement with his arm. Ron was in the zone.

After the performance, Ron gave me the tour of the shop. As we stepped into the infamous back room, I was amazed. There was a jukebox, tables and chairs and four of the coolest pinball machines I had ever seen. They were alive, lights blinking, grinding and whirling noises. One even spoke to us: "Howdy partner, want to try your luck?" It was incredible. You could select your favorite song on the jukebox and be playing right along. I walked up, caressed one of the machines and checked out the selections on the jukebox.

The final section of the store was the Employees Only inner sanctum: Accounting, corporate boardroom (bathroom) and storage area. Ron introduced me to three members of the team, Chuck, Bob and Bill. Chuck ran the store in Rockville and had been with Empire for many years. Bob was largely responsible for the management of the machines, evidenced by his large collection of keys on his belt that jingled at every move. He showed an obvious pride in their possession, and he spoke in a voice of authority. Bill quickly reached out his hand and said, "Hi. Everyone calls me Junior." Junior and I would become the best of friends.

I took in the surroundings and marveled at the early-basement design theme. It had the old sofa; the broken office chair, missing a wheel; and boxes and boxes of overstock records and tapes, the old sales signs, out-of-date promotional posters and the stacks of albums staging for the next $1.99 sale.

Off in the corner, away from the storage, sat a slender woman, head down, mulling over register receipt after receipt from the five stores in the chain. Rose was the financial department of the organization. Her rants were legendary, always including "Boat load of shit" and repeated use of the word "Fuck"—not what I was used to from a woman a few years older, but an entertaining spectacle nonetheless.

In Empire Music, I entered a forbidden world, and I loved it all.

Ron and I were sitting in the Quad, likely the next day, when I asked him if there were any openings at Empire.

He said he would check.

A few days later, I found myself face-to-face with owner Jim Seward. At 6 feet 2 inches, 150 pounds and dressed in all black, he reminded me of Johnny Cash. He had a stringy beard, long straight hair and had obviously had bad acne when he was much younger. His mannerisms were a challenge in eye contact. Jim would stare, then avert his eyes up and to the side, so he was hard to follow. There was also the constant sniffling as though he had post-nasal drip.

My interview didn't last long.

"Where did you grow up?" he asked.

"Over off River Road across from Kenwood Country Club," I answered.

Jim nodded his head. "What kind of student are you?" he continued.

"I got straight A's in seventh grade. Ever since, it's been mostly C's."

"Why is that?"

I shrugged.

Then there was the big question: "Why do you want to work in my record store?"

"I think it would be a blast," I replied, and he smiled.

We talked about hours, what I would be doing, and he used the word flunky, which didn't feel so great, but Jim obviously liked the sound of it. He asked about my favorite rock bands, which included quite a list.

After a short pause, he asked, "You want the job?"

I said yes.

A DEAL'S A DEAL

The job was heaven. I felt like a grown up. Even better, I felt like I was part of the Empire.

The Empire had several parts. The Rockville store across from Gaithersburg High School was run by Bob, a regimented guy, who I thought was a Marine. It was uneventful in comparison to the second store in Bethesda, a small shop alongside a "head shop" and across from Tastee Diner, a Bethesda landmark. This store was run by Nick Chaconas, yes, from WHMC fame.

Traversing the many store locations was commonplace. Starting in Bethesda and being remanded to Silver Spring was just the beginning. I loved visiting the Georgetown location, a busy store in an always crowded neighborhood with lots of young people from two universities. That was always an event for people watching.

I must have been a fairly good assistant manager, because Jim seemed to trust me. I spent more and more time with him. Soon, he moved me from the Bethesda mother store to the run-down Silver Spring store.

Jim loved to tell stories, and part of the reason I visited the Bethesda store so often was to listen to him. He was an irrepressible character.

The classic stories of the early years included antics from motorcycle rides in pajamas with an attractive passenger around the sidewalks of Congressional Plaza to the Cadillac story. That was my favorite.

Jim must have been in his late 20s or very early 30s, a few years into the record business, and 1968 must have been a good year. He made a prank of his visit to Suburban Cadillac on Arlington Road, dressing in a torn, ragged-collared shirt along with a pair of pants last worn to paint the store interior. Suburban Cadillac was one of those places most people did not feel confident enough to enter no matter how well dressed. Jim was not most people.

In the store's all-glass showroom, he was soon drooling over a new Cadillac Eldorado. He was in love. It was pearl white, sleek lines with a notched back, and, of course, that long hood. It was sex on wheels for Jim.

In most cases a salesman would have approached like a pelican: a brief recon circle, then the dive to the target. But in Jim's case, the sales force, less than enticed by his appearance, had little confidence he would produce a sale.

Jim says, "Hey, how much is this car?"

The salesman yells across the showroom, "It's $6,600."

Jim says, "Does that include taxes and tags?"

The increasingly irritated salesman, sure there is no way this guy is going to buy this car, looks at his colleague, smirks and says, "Yea, sure buddy, taxes and tags included."

Jim says, "So what if I needed the front seat moved back a few inches, that included?"

The sales guy, enjoying his joke says, "Sure buddy, it's all included."

Jim reaches into his baggy trousers, pulls out $6,600 in cash and waves it in the air. "OK, I got it right here," he says.

The sales guy, in total disbelief at seeing this big wad of bills, rushes over, now just like a pelican, and grabs the wad, looking initially as though it must be from a Monopoly game. It wasn't.

"I didn't think you were serious. I mean look at yourself. You have to realize that I didn't really mean all those things were included, right?"

Jim says, "a deal's a deal."

He would have driven it away but first the front seat had to be moved back nine inches. In this and all his subsequent Cadillacs, Jim looked like he was driving lying down.

The more time I spent listening to Jim, the more he trusted me, the more I got to do. Soon, I was doing things I'd never imagined, and pulling them off.

SINGING ON THE RADIO

He even trusted me with store advertising.

"This has got to be one of your dumber ideas," Junior said. After five or six months of working together, Junior and I were pretty tight. A lot of our cleverer schemes, we did together.

"I mean you really think this is going to work, us singing this crap on the radio?"

"Yea, I do," I said. "I think this thing is going to sound so bad everyone will remember it. So, let's go over it again."

We must have both been a bit nervous, having never done a commercial on the radio before, but here we were.

Empire had been advertising on local radio stations for years. This was our chance to put a new face on the advertising. I must have pitched the idea to Jim, and he thought it was great. He trusted me, a 17-year-old kid, at the altar of the cathedral of my generation.

For the rebellious era of the 1960s, music was like life itself. Growing up, we kids ran away from the Top 40 radio stations like WINX and WHOL and into the arms of WHMC and WHFS. I am not sure how I found these stations earlier, either stumbling on them or learning about them through talk from friends, then searching the bandwidth late at night for the small signals. But find them I did, and in them I took refuge.

We were pretty raw when we headed out the next morning to WHMC. Located in the midst of a cow field and surrounded by lush vegetation was a small cinderblock building that certainly was not my idea of a radio station. But a large broadcast tower loomed right next to the cinderblock building, so it had to be.

Most of us that grew up in Bethesda in the late 1960s remember WHMC and its outspoken, larger than life DJ, Barry Richards. The lead-in to his show, sung by some female voices, went something like "Barry Richards Show on the Radio, Barry Richards Show on the Radio." He would end his broadcast with "you may be the flower, but I'm the root" and other catchy phrases like "I am the Boss with the Hot Sauce."

WHMC was an AM radio station. Its biggest competition was WHFS, an FM station in the heart of Bethesda. Barry said, "as far as I'm concerned, FM means Find Me."

We all knew who Barry Richards was, and we lived and died by his radio show.

So WHMC's studio was something of a disappointment. I was still fascinated. The broadcast studio looked like someone's basement, full of electronic gear with a large microphone stuck in the middle. The studio where we cut the commercial was smaller still, a large mixing board surrounded by large stacks of tape recording machines on top of one another, not at all like what you'd see on TV. The scene aligned with *pay no attention to the man behind the curtain* from the *Wizard of Oz*.

It was about right for the commercial we cut, which was as bad as we could make it. We'd figured we'd never succeed with a good one, so we took the opposite tack.

After the first take Nick Chaconas, the owner, said, "that sucked."

He was right, so we couldn't argue, and he was trying to be helpful.

"Let's take a couple minutes and try again," he said. "You two look like you didn't get much sleep last night.

What I do when I'm feeling like that, is to go in the men's room, splash water on my face and then rub my face with a couple paper towels, vigorously. It wakes me right up."

Junior and I just stared at each other thinking, "Is this real?"

"Come on, let's try it," he said.

So we gave it a shot. He led the way to the men's room and demonstrated what he was talking about, the water, the aggressive rubbing of faces. I was thankful there were two of us.

The second take was a keeper.

"Much better," Mr. C said, "let's put this on a cart and que it up right away."

The next thing I know, we're on the radio singing "Empire Music in Bethesda, Empire Music in Gaithersburg, Empire Music in Georgetown..."

It wasn't long before people would walk into the store singing this jingle, and yes, it was terrible.

My return trips to WHMC for subsequent commercials were largely unsupervised, which afforded me opportunity to experiment and be creative. One commercial had the voice of The Shadow and a creepy laugh with a reverb. It sounded cool: "Who knows what records and tapes lurk at Empire Music? The Shadow knows...hooooah ha ha ha." That was by far my favorite.

Making commercials at WHFS-FM was a different ball game. Both stations were progressive, but otherwise they were as unlike as a Volkswagen Bug and a Cadillac. WHFS-FM was a very professional set up, a separate studio for the engineer and another for the person being recorded. They treated me like a 17-year-old kid.

So my first experience there was shocking. Having cut the spot, I was relieved. But then came another round of listening and being prompted by the engineer, then corrected and coached. Ten takes nearly put me over the edge, and I didn't see much difference between the first and the last.

I headed back to the store to complain with Rose. Before I knew it, Jim was motioning me into the conference room. The conference room was really the bathroom, which was only a sink and toilet, but it was the only private room in the whole store. To use this with two people inside was intimate. One person had to straddle the john while the other stood with their back to the sink.

"What happened at HFS?" Jim said.

"I could be exaggerating, but the engineer was not very accommodating," I said. "I felt that he treated me like a child."

Jim's face grew red and his common sniffling reached an epic frequency.

"I own that place over there," he said...

...I was sure he meant figuratively. I knew Jake Einstein owned the station.

"I pump a lot of money in there, and the next time Einstein wants my help he can go fuck himself."

I had not seen Jim this pissed off before.

"If this happens again," he fumed, "you tell me right away."

Conference over, Jim calmed down and we exited the conference room, which I was glad of since the up-close proximity was starting to bug me.

The next time I visited the station to cut a commercial, things were very much improved.

Still, I preferred hanging out at WHMC. I could walk right into the broadcast studio through the rear door and strike up a conversation with Barry Richards or Billy Chaconas, Nick's son and another DJ. You had to be quiet and respectful and wait until a commercial or record was playing; you couldn't just start talking unless you wanted to become part of the broadcast. But the atmosphere was much more relaxed and fun.

At WHFS I don't think I ever met anyone when I was making commercials. Cerphe, Weasel and the other DJs were always quarantined in the broadcast studio, an isolated room and not easily accessible to someone just walking in.

The two stations were kind of like the difference between pumping your own gas and having an attendant do it for you. You lost the experience of the act and could only watch while someone else performed it.

In a few months at Empire Music, I'd gotten used to doing it all on my own.

What more could a 1960s' high school kid want? Jim Seward was my idol.

MEETING THE BETHESDA BOMBER

"Hey, look at this magazine," Jim Seward called out. "This is a bit of my younger years."

There on the pages of *True Detective* crime magazine was Jim's picture with the caption—I read it out-loud—"Bethesda Youth Arrested for Local Bombings." I looked up to see a wide smile across Jim's face. "This was you?" I asked.

"Yea, when I was in high school, I went to school one day and was sent to the principal's office for wearing Levis—not allowed in Bethesda-Chevy Chase High School. Mr. Zimmerman sent me home to change. Boy that really pissed me off. I was so angry."

"What happened after that?" I asked.

"I went to his house that night and blew it up," Seward trumpeted. "I'd made sure nobody was home. It was quite the spectacle. Man you should have seen it," he proudly said.

"Jesus!" I said, "You blew his house up?"

"Yea, he pissed me off. I blew up the library too."

"What?" I said, at the top of my voice. "Jesus, Jim!"

"I went to return a book that was a bit overdue," he recounted. "The woman in the library gave me so much shit about how I was irresponsible and didn't care about the rules, she just went on and on. I didn't deserve that. I mean I brought the f'ing book back didn't I? She said she was going to alert my teacher. Well I came back to the library that night after dark and I lit it up, it was a gorgeous fire, every fire truck for miles was there."

Holy mother of god, I had never met anyone like this. Sure I read about them, but here I was standing face to face with an honest-to-god bomber, and he seemed really excited about it. "So that was it?" I asked. "Only the two bombings?"

"No, no," he said. "There were others. They didn't catch us for all of them. One night we were at the Hot Shoppes drive-in, Old Georgetown Road and Wisconsin Avenue, minding our own business when this waitress skates up to our car door and starts complaining about how loud our radio is. She starts in about what a mess we were making spilling all the stuff off our car tray onto the ground. I mean, really?" he said in protest.

"Then the manager comes out to make an appearance and reinforce what the car hop had said. Something clicked in my brain, it seemed excessive, maybe the resistance to authority, not sure, but later that night after they closed up, I came back and blew it up."

Jim had become quite animated and excited, squirming and jerking, and yes, the snorting and sniffling was much more pronounced.

"Boy, you were on quite the streak, principal's house, library and Hot Shoppes?" I reflected, "What would have been next? I mean did you have a plan?"

"Yea," he said, "we had the mother of all targets as one of the next, the Bethesda Police Station on Elm Street. Now that would have gotten Cronkite's attention and made the *Evening News*."

"So what happened?" I asked.

"We got arrested," he sadly admitted. "Once we were in the system, it took a whole different direction, our parents freaked, they hired lawyers, you know, a downward spiral."

In custody, Jim was held at the Loch Raven Maryland Training School, where he later served time. He'd been sentenced as a juvenile, so he made it out "free, white and 21," as he had planned.

His first job out of prison was working for his father, a plumbing contractor. He described the endless days and days of digging ditches and laying pipe and how much he disliked it. He knew there was a different life than this, and he created it in Empire Music.

MEETING THE FBI

Jim Seward was a well-known son of Bethesda. He had spent his whole life there, and his father owned JP Seward Plumbing Company. Both embedded Jim in the history of this town. He was also embedded in the files of the Federal Bureau of Investigation. Because of Jim's flamboyant past career, the minute there was any suspicious act of arson or an unexplained explosion, the FBI would show up, always in pairs, always in dark suits.

I was working in the Bethesda store one afternoon after school when in walked two men in business suits and hats. (It has been said that John Kennedy killed the hat industry by not wearing a hat at his inauguration, but these gentlemen had not gotten the memo.)

"Is Jim Seward here?" one asked.

I didn't put all of this together initially. "I'll have to check. Can I tell him who's here?" I said trying to muster some authority while looking at Ron to give me some direction.

"Just tell him we have some questions we need to ask him."

I guessed that was part of the we-ask-the-questions-we-don't-answer-them strategy. Being 17 and not having much confidence, and getting no indicators from Ron, I retreated to the back-room office and told Jim that he had some visitors in suits.

"Shit," he said, "not again."

"What do they want?" he said in the same way a parent would grill you.

"He said they have questions," I said. That was the best answer I had.

I followed several steps behind in the migration out into the store and the waiting duo.

"I'm Jim Seward," he announced.

"Mr. Seward, I'm Agent Wallace and this is Agent Ashley. Can you tell us your whereabouts on Tuesday the 18th from 5 p.m. to 10 p.m.?"

"I was at my apartment in the Washingtonian Towers," Jim replied.

"Were you alone or can someone corroborate your story?" Wallace said matter-of-factly.

"No, I was alone," Jim offered. "Why all the questions?"

"We'll ask the questions," Wallace said.

(I had been waiting for this exchange.)

"Look, if you guys can't give me any info, then I think we're done here," Jim said.

"That's fine, Mr. Seward. We have a few more questions, but if you would rather answer them downtown, we can make that happen," Wallace said, too soothingly.

"Alright, alright, let's take a seat," Jim said.

The conversation and the questions continued, and though I couldn't hear most of the words, I got the sentiments of the back and forth. Wallace would ask the questions and Jim would shake his head and deny any knowledge of the event in question. At one point Wallace would say something to the effect of "Well, we just thought that someone with your colorful background might have some information we don't currently have."

"No," Jim said. "That was a long time ago."

With no fruit on the tree, the agents seemed to lose what enthusiasm they had.

As they cleared the door, Jim muttered under his breath, "I hate those mother f**ckers."

This was my very first experience with Jim's notoriety, but it would not be the last.

Later that day, Jim brought the BSA triple-cylinder motorcycle out of the back room and through the store.

"I need to get some air after that," he said.

He was dating a woman named Brenda, from the Bethesda store. She was just about as tall as Jim and, by anybody's description, a knockout. She was probably 10 years younger than Jim, but it did not seem to matter to anyone, least of all Jim. They seemed inseparable, and they were, until, I guess, they weren't.

He gave Brenda leave to quit work for the day. They hopped on, Jim slid a .38 snub nose into his jacket pocket, saying "just in case we run into any Pagans." And away they went in a whoosh of throaty exhaust.

Growing up in Bethesda, I knew the Pagan motorcycle gang was the East Coast equivalent of the Hells Angels. I would later meet Fat Freddy and hear stories about his good friend Beach Ball as well as Little Jesus. In later years I would end up with Fat Freddie's three-cylinder Triumph motorcycle and be invited to join the Hyattsville Chapter by Vice President Richard Day. Even at that open-minded time, I didn't go for the urine-soaked-garment initiation. Stepping aside was one of my good calls. Many of these guys, including Fat Freddy, ended up going away for many years.

MEETING THE MUSIC MAKERS

Working in the Empire opened my world to all kinds of celebrities.

Junior walked into the store exclaiming, "I've got the back-stage passes."

"You're shitting me," I said.

"No, right here. You and I, my man, are going to rub elbows with John Kay and Steppenwolf at Cole Field House in College Park."

Steppenwolf had three top hits in 1968, "Born to be Wild," "Magic Carpet Ride" and the all-time favorite "The Pusher," maybe my favorite. The promise of actually attending a rock concert and being allowed back stage was a dream come true. I was beyond excited and couldn't wait until Saturday.

Junior had one of the first Ford Mustang sedans, complete with a 260 V8 engine. He would unselfishly allow me to drive on occasion; the fact that I did not have a permit seemed unimportant. So we arrived at Cole Field House in style.

At the hall, we went to the side-stage entrance. The crowd was already about 90 percent in attendance, and the din in the room was loud. You could feel the energy and anticipation of the upcoming performance.

We were checked into the back-stage area and led to a large room where the entire band was hanging out. I was overcome with excitement; I felt like I was in a dream. The unreality expanded when we were introduced to John Kay, the lead singer. Famous as he was, he was very friendly. Junior, the conversationalist, started by complimenting the band and its string of recent hits. I was in shock and could not find my voice.

John told us that the band only worked on weekends. I thought that was so cool. Looking around the room, I saw that what ever you were thinking would be good to snack on was here and ready. Do you party before or after, or maybe both? I wondered. How this all worked was a mystery to me.

The concert was amazing and, yes, all the hot numbers were covered in a thrilling on-stage fashion:

smoke, lights, the light show with food coloring and oil on an overhead projector, a trick I never tired of. After the two-hour show, John and the band headed for the rear door and into an awaiting limousine, which whisked them away. I did not ask what the destination was, but I was sure the party would take on a very different focus now that the show was behind them.

I went home that night sad at what else new and wonderful we were missing.

The shows and access continued. I met some of the greats of the age: Grace Slick, Janis Joplin and Tom Rush. With the back-and-forth on the road, substance in a conversation is rare; you don't expect it. A real connection is even rarer. I mean most of these folks are meeting thousands of people over the course of a tour, and it would not be very realistic to expect a deep relationship developing from a few minutes of polite conversation. I still enjoyed it immensely and valued each and every iteration.

But in rare occasions there would actually be substantive and moving conversation. I remember meeting Richie Havens at the no-longer-there Cellar Door in Georgetown and having what felt at the time to be a deeper-than-normal conversation about his challenges and performance beginnings.

Richie had a unique music style that combined with his gravely voice and guitar tunings to make him easily recognizable regardless of the song. He also seemed to be uncommonly thoughtful, as well as accessible. As I understand it, during the 1969 Woodstock Music Festival, the traffic was so jammed that many performers were delayed in their arrivals. Richie played for hours to keep the crowd engaged until other acts arrived. His Woodstock performance of "Freedom" was stunning. *Freedom, freedom...some times I feel like a motherless child, far far from my home*. What a bone-rattling song.

MEETING MY FUTURE

"My girlfriend's pregnant," I said to Jim.

"Don't worry," Peggy, aka Squeak, had said when she showed up at the Bethesda store to tell me the news. "I've arranged to have an abortion."

"Wow, is there anything I can do to help?" I said.

"I don't think so," she replied. "Maybe we'll see each other again," she said as she left.

What a shitty feeling that was for us both.

I had to tell somebody, so I'd worked up the courage to tell Jim.

He paused for a long moment, then motioned toward the chairs in the Bethesda store's pinball annex.

Mid-morning, before the school-skippers arrived, the room was nearly empty and the pinballs and jukebox quiet. We sat down.

"You dig Squeak?" he asked.

"Yes," I said.

"She dig you?" he continued.

"Yes."

"Then what's the problem?" Jim said.

He added this prediction to put his advice in perspective: "Someday, Randy, you are going to have your own business, and somebody that works for you is going to come up and say, 'hey my girlfriend's pregnant.'"

I thought, yea, right! As it turns out he was pretty darn close, not word for word, but pretty darn close.

This was a defining moment in my relationship with Jim, maybe for the ability to discuss a life-changing event with each other, or maybe because I had grown up a bit.

Jim and I seemed to grow close over our time together. He invited me to his apartment on the 16th floor of the Washingtonian Towers, maybe the first high rise of its kind built in the middle of a golf course. Jim did not play golf.

The views were amazing, looking out over Route 270 and off in the distance, the Bethesda Naval

Hospital tower and parts of Bethesda: stunning. The interior was well done, even professional, and I suppose plush. Two leather reclining chairs in front of the TV and a small dinette off the living room, nice kitchen and a powder room. The bedroom and private bath were around the corner, and were also well appointed, the carpet was very plush and his stereo and TV were state-of-the-art for the time, It was a true bachelor pad to envy.

But my favorite interior element was the one-armed bandit slot machine off the dining room. It was a 10-cent machine, and I was dying to play it. Jim quickly pointed out that even though there was a small dish of dimes, all winnings stayed with, and in, the house. I was a bit deflated by that news, but not discouraged enough to not play after permission was granted. It was a blast, the whirring sound, the gears turning, and on occasion, a modest contribution to keep me engaged. Clack, whirr, clunk, clunk, clunk, I loved it. I wanted one.

On a later visit to the apartment, with Jim driving his Cadillac, we passed the entrance to the highrise and headed to the rear parking lot. He pulled up to a collection of Lincoln Continentals, all nested together. There was the iconic 1965 Continental with the famous suicide doors alongside a 1958 Mark II, and to round things out a two-door version of the Mark II.

Yes, Jim was a gear head. "Riding in those is like sitting in your living room on a sofa," he said. "They hardly move or rock at all, A lovely automobile!" he said.

"Those are yours?" I asked.

"Yes," he said. "I've had them for a while, need to get them fixed up."

I was getting to know Jim pretty well, but we'd never done drugs together until out of the blue, he said, "We're going to do a store move tonight. Want to come?"

As he said this, he held out his hand filled with Black Beauties, methamphetamine, a popular pick-me-up of the day.

This was my introduction to a tried-and-true ritual of Empire's history.

The Georgetown store on M Street stayed open until midnight. We showed up after closing and went to work emptying the record bins and pulling up the carpet. The objective was to redo the store overnight and open the next day.

This store was my favorite of the chain. It was so small you needed a shoe horn to get to the back. But it was magic. On many a night, I would come down and hang out. On a good night you could hear the music blaring and thumping as you rounded the Northwest corner of Wisconsin and M Street, and it only got louder as you passed the stores next door, Up Against The Wall and Elysian Fields.

Mike Burke, the manager-in-charge, was an unmistakable individual. He had a thick and long head of hair similar to a lion's mane, on top of a very slender body, kind of a human Pez dispenser. Mike had been at the helm for years and seemed to have his own source of Black Beauties, which he carried in a leather pouch tied to his belt.

The whole evening was quite bizarre, the lead up, the invitation and now no Mike. What I didn't know was that I was smack in the middle of a regime change. Mike was out.

As the night dragged on and the work continued, the pills were plentiful. Out of the blue, Jim called Junior aside.

"I want you to take over this store," Jim said.

Junior looked shocked, and he was.

He and I had been making plans to leave town. The idea was to head to Fayetteville, North Carolina, to visit Junior's parents, then onward to try for jobs at Southeastern Record Distributors in Charlotte, where

Empire purchased all the records sold in the store. We'd told nobody anything, including our plan to leave the very next day.

"I'd love to, Jim, but I've got a job lined up at Southeastern."

Now it was Jim's turn to be shocked. "I was not expecting you to say that," he told Junior, pissed.

He turned to me. "And you, what are your plans?"

"I'm going with Junior."

Boy that did not play well at all. Jim whipped out a big wad of cash and paid us off, on the spot. "I guess we're done here," he raged. "Get the fuck out!"

The trip to North Carolina didn't go as I planned. We made it to Junior's parents all right, and that's where Squeak's mother caught up with me.

She showed up in a fury, dragging Squeak, who was Peggy to her and obviously had not had an abortion. Mrs. Vreeland had it all arranged, and her threat of a paternity suit brought me into the plan. Squeak and I got married in Dillon, South Carolina, where legal age was 18.

Maybe a year later, after welcoming a child, I came back to the Empire. I needed a job, and Jim actually hired me back. But it was not the same.

It lasted maybe a year and ended with a Last Lunch.

Jim walked into the Gaithersburg store and said, "let's get some lunch." He was pissed off, agitated, short on words, and I knew something was up.

"Get anything you want on the menu."

"Really?" I said, "Anything?"

"Sure," he said.

There was no mistake. You know sometimes, you just have a feeling, that something is terribly wrong and about to get much worse. This was one of those times.

"I really don't like the way that you've been putting the signs up in the window," he said. "The tape is all wrong. It should be parallel to the sign, not perpendicular. I just hate that."

I'm hearing Rod Serling in the back of my head as the syncopated music starts in, *duda, duda, duda, duda...* "You're traveling through another dimension, a dimension not only of sight and sound but of mind..."

Boy this was totally out of the *Twilight Zone*, but I kept it together even though my head was spinning and my pulse rate had doubled.

"Seriously, Jim?"

"Yes, it's all wrong, I had high hopes when you came back, but it just hasn't worked out," he said.

The food, a cheeseburger, arrived but my appetite had already gone. I didn't know what to say, maybe because I had never been fired before, but here it was. I got up and left.

A couple years after I had left Empire, I stopped at the store.

Jim introduced his new wife, Marian. She was the daughter of Al Derr, of Al's Deli next door to the Old Georgetown Road store. I'm guessing Jim was around 34 when I came to work at Empire. When I met Jim's 14-year-old wife, I think he was 36. Apparently Al had given permission for Marian and Jim to wed. As a wedding present, Jim bought each of them matching Fleetwood Cadillacs.

I think the marriage lasted only a few months.

TAKING THE BUS

Periodically, I stopped by Empire with Squeak, who by now was again Peggy. On one occasion, after our son Jason was born, we asked Jim to be his godfather. I think Jim was taken aback, probably a new role for him. In any event, he readily agreed. He showed up for the christening, yes, in a Cadillac, and with a bright smile. It was a good day.

On maybe the last time I saw Jim, he had permed his hair.

"When did you change the hairdo?" I asked.

"I wanted to look like you," he said, somewhat sarcastically.

Jim and I had put quite a bit of distance between us from the early days. I suppose the expectations had never been correctly aligned, and were now adrift even more.

It was maybe four years after I had left Empire that I heard Jim had "taken the bus," as many people in that depressed state call suicide. He was 40. The apple and the tree: It made me think of Jim's mother and him finding her when he was only 11, when she had hung herself in the bathroom.

Always the considerate individual, Jim had sat in the bathtub in his apartment, taken his .38 and blown a hole through his head and the bathroom tile. It was three days before new girlfriend, Maryanne, found him.

Tragedy, prison, substance abuse and self-medication, the failed relationships: Jim's life did not seem as glamorous as it once did to a 17-year-old boy.

Yet I still feel an emptiness today.

ENTERPRISE WOODCRAFT & DESIGN COMPANY

1979

I had been working for my wife Peggy's uncle as a cabinetmaker and woodworker for a few years when, one Friday in 1979, I asked Uncle Doug if I could cut my hours back to 32 per week.

"Why would you want to only work 32 hours in a week?" he said.

Being naive, I went with the honest approach: "I can make more money doing side work, so fewer hours here would let me have another day of side work."

Uncle Doug thought a minute about this proposition before answering. "How about we cut your hours back to zero. How would that be?"

I wasn't prepared for that possibility. I was caught off guard, and it kind of made me angry. But I pulled it together and said, "Yea, that would work, definitely."

So much for my becoming a partner. Uncle Doug had tantalized me with that possibility—then pulled it back.

"I've thought about it, but I just don't think it would work," he said. "You are very moody, and you work all the time. Why don't you stop working so much, join the country club and play some golf?"

I mean it's not like I had all this extra money lying around.

Now, in the space of a few minutes, I had gone into business for myself. Twenty-five years old, married, three kids, a mortgage—yeah, you got it, insane.

This scenario has been a repeating theme for me. Anger has propelled me for a good part of my life. It is an effective strategy, but I wouldn't recommend it.

1970

Peggy and I had met back in 1968 when I was working in Empire Music in Silver Spring. One thing led to another, and we became a couple. It didn't last long. After I had transferred to another of the five stores, Peggy showed up and announced that she was [we were] pregnant. Boy, the adrenaline, elevated heart rate and spinning series of thoughts was intense.

"You want to keep it?" I asked.

"No, I'm getting an abortion. A friend has a friend that can help," she said.

Relief? Maybe, but still crazy. "Well, can I help, anything I can do?" I asked.

"Nope, I'll see you around," she said. And she was gone.

What in the world? An 18-year-old high school dropout, and almost a father.

A few months later, as I was heading out to Charlotte, North Carolina, to work at a record distributor, Peggy showed up, obviously pregnant. We got married and had two more children.

1968

High school was a complete bore to me. The exception was one week in 11th grade of a test curriculum, called Experiment in Free Form Education week or EFFE. All students could create their own schedule from a list of alternative classes. It seemed too good to be true. You mean no French, no algebra? The luxury of picking your own curriculum and classes was fantastic. If it had become a new structure, I might have just stuck around.

English class with Dr. Boyle was not my favorite. I had handed in some poems as extra credit. Perhaps I was too naive; when I got them back they were all marked up with red ink. Such a disappointment.

I suppose I was hoping for something positive, or maybe encouraging.

"What about the content?" I asked.

"I am grading on structure, format, punctuation and grammar," Dr. Boyle responded.

Much later in life, I learned that you can't hold someone accountable for something you haven't taught or communicated to them.

That day, Dr. Boyle had other bad news. "Randy, you have been summoned to Mr. Donovans' office," he said.

You know that surge of adrenaline. "You have been summoned..." Holy shit, am I in bad trouble? Probably.

My father was waiting with Mr. Donovan in the guidance counselor's office. Mr. Donovan, an average-looking guy with a sports coat and a mop haircut, my father in his typical suit and tie with a more-than-acceptably short, slicked-back hairstyle.

"Come on in, Randy. Your father and I have been discussing your attendance challenges. Here, have a seat," Mr. Donovan said. (Oh great, a tag-team match, wtf.)

"Well, Randy," Mr. Donovan started, "as you are aware, you have skipped almost half your classes. Your father and I are concerned. What are you doing when you're skipping class?" he asked.

"I'm usually working at the record store," I answered.

"Your father and I feel you need to make a choice, going to school or working in the record store."

"Well, that's not a hard decision," I said. "I'll work in the record store."

The look of oh, shit was all over both their faces, not the way they were hoping things would go after that brilliant presentation. They had missed on this one.

The record store was exciting, interesting and a whole lot more fun than going to algebra or most other classes. Hated French. Art was OK (actually was introduced to pottery there), but for the most part the store was cool.

1980
R.T. ESTABROOK CO.

So what do you do when you find you are going into business?

Good question.

I had been introduced to the Architectural Woodwork Institute around that time and found it a wealth of information and opportunity. Member firms across the United States were in the architectural woodworking industry.

I know, what's that?

Most people ask if you make kitchen cabinets, and most firms do. However, there are a plethora of other offerings, expertise and capabilities. Think of a nice building lobby in a metropolitan downtown area, think of the reception desk, any displays and of course the wood-veneer wall surfacing all around the lobby. Include in this list restaurant interiors, department stores, shopping malls and you start to get the possible scope of such a firm. All of these items come from a firm that produces architectural woodwork.

As long as I was going into business for myself, I might as well do what I liked: architectural woodwork.

Having spent some time in a couple makeshift shops, I was bitten. I loved the challenge of figuring out how to transform the image on paper into a three-dimensional form. In some cases the paper image posed a number of challenges, but wading through and solving the problems was the best. It allowed me to be a part of the design process, the solving and making.

Early pursuits were a cedar chest for my sister, a cradle for one of my little ones and a dry sink for a friend. The list of possibilities was endless, and that was a good thing.

I was going to make cool stuff—once I figured out where. I started with a simple criterion: not too far away from home.

The space I settled on was a petite 1,200 square-foot rectangle, about twice as big as a two-car garage, on Warren Street in Silver Spring. It was an old Quonset hut, pretty cheap, all metal cladding, no insulation.

That would become a real issue when winter came. R. T. Estabrook Co. shared the Quonset hut with a firewood company and a general contractor, S&M.

In setting up the shop, my inexperience and naïveté were in full swing. I looked at ads in the paper for used machinery and went to look at different items. For a used table saw, in reasonable shape, I paid way too much. For small hand tools like routers, jig saws, drills, I opted for mostly Sears-brand items. They weren't the best but would do. Later, tools would be upgraded to much better models.

So plug the tools in and start making stuff, right? It's a bit more complicated. First you need to find something to build, preferably for money.

A friend was moving his flower shop to a new location. That became my first project. I knew that with any project, you need to break down the items to be built and create drawings, showing dimensions and details such as joinery, with, of course, a materials list. Next you combine information, materials and talent to start the project.

Starting a project without defining any one of these necessities is sure to result in derailment. I was lucky at the flower shop. As the business grew, I started a few projects without a full list so I could keep the craftsmen busy. But I soon learned I didn't want to rely on luck when I was making ungainly, multi-thousand dollar projects.

On an early credenza project with matching wall cabinet for a law office, we had, for whatever reason, made the hanging wall unit in one long assembled length, 12 feet long. We were so proud and thought we were so smart by making this thing in one piece.

As I pulled the truck up to the building entrance, it hit me like a tennis racket hitting a ball. Not all elevator cabs are 12 feet tall. Most elevators in commercial buildings are only about eight to nine feet tall inside the cab. I turned in panic to my second employee, Wayne.

"Shit, I did not check the size of the elevator," he said. "How are we gonna get this thing up there? He's on the eighth floor. I mean we can't even take it up the stairwell."

"I think we might be screwed on this one," I admitted. "Did we bring a handsaw? Maybe we could saw the thing in half."

With a sinking feeling of dread, we walked up to the elevator and pushed the button. The doors started to slide open like the curtains on the stage of a play. I looked inside, and I could not believe my luck. The cab was 12 feet tall. It would fit. Again, I was lucky.

PARTNERSHIP

But luck and artistry were not enough to see me through my first year. Having started my business without much knowledge of business, both undercapitalized and naive, I soon realized that applying what I had observed in other shops was not enough. Enter our Quonset neighbors Steve and Marvin: S&M.

S&M had been in business for several years, and once they saw how rapidly we progressed on a bookcase job they'd given us, they were impressed, as if we had a hidden set of elves, for the bookcases seemed to almost assemble themselves.

After almost 11 months, my erosion of funds led me into partnership with Steve and Marvin.

Steve was a tall, dark-haired, medium-built guy with a hint of Middle Eastern heritage. He was friendly but very serious when it came to business. Steve's strengths were good ones: managing projects and watching the money.

Marvin was blond, average height and very stocky. You could tell from his thick arms and upper chest that he had spent some time in the gym. His strengths were hands-on. He knew how to build things, so well that it was hard for him to take a hands-off approach to delegating.

Over the next four to five years, I learned quite a bit about running a company and being a boss. Both men were pretty good teachers, and they were invested in our shared success. Working with them was my college education.

"You know, Randy," Steve said, "You can't keep getting high with everyone that works for you."

"Why not?" I asked.

"Because one day you might need to fire them," Steve said.

I had not considered this very real possibility, and he was right. Having gotten high together would make things much more difficult on an emotional level.

In those early years I had only a couple of people working for me. I'd placed classified ads in *The Washington Post* and made lucky hires. Both were skilled and easy to work with, the kind of guys you'd want to share a joint with.

Paul was a good woodworker and an odd character. A heavy-to-average built towheaded guy, he was born an albino. His biggest challenge was the lack of pigment in his eyes, making him have to study things at very close range. Paul was also quite animated, and he loved certain phrases such as "he's got five pounds of shit in a one-pound bag." This statement caused periodic contemplation. His other favorite phrase was "leaping screaming ___!" Insert your own final word, such as "That is leaping screaming crazy!"

Dwayne was a lanky dark-haired guy with a scruffy beard. His mannerisms were quirky, and he was overflowing with nervous energy, making him quite productive. As a woodworker, Dwayne brought us some of the best skills I had seen so far on this journey. At a restaurant we were working on, Dwayne showed us all how to build up strip-wood laminations to produce radiused-bullnose details on sections of the bar.

We had evolved from the restaurant job to building several stores in the then new Georgetown Park development in Washington, D.C. One store was Natural Cosmetics, a sea of white laminate bookcases and a matching cash and wrap counter with display. This was a fairly straightforward project, except we were behind schedule and the mall had a drop-dead opening date.

"We will not miss that opening date," said Judith Miller, who owned the franchise. The wife of D.C. developer Stuart Miller of the Miller Companies, Judith was exacting. It was a long 36 straight hours of installation to pull it off. The three of us were exhausted, but we got it open on time.

We built a fruit-and-nut store on the lower level that was made entirely out of mahogany—hanging signs, display cases, countertops: It was beautiful!

As part of the journey, I remember that we had to make some 4-inch crown molding out of mahogany to trim the upper perimeter of the fruit and nut kiosk. No problem, right? Well, yes, problem. We did not have a shaper, much less shaper knives to make the molding. A trip to Baltimore to buy a new Powermatic shaper was the first step.

Next, I needed a 4-inch knife for this profile. The expert in wood work was old man Wagner, and I was a regular customer at his mill in Rockville. I asked him how to grind the knife I needed. "Yea, that's a tough one to start out with," he said.

Yea, you bet! I asked a lot of questions to a series of folks and ultimately ground the knives myself. Getting the undulating profile on one knife was not the worst part, but getting the second knife to more or less match the first knife was a lot more difficult.

I ground the profile out of 3-to-4 inch lock-edge pieces of steel, then put the two knives in a collar that fits over a round spindle in the shaper. Then the moment of truth. I placed a big piece of wood up on the table of the shaper to block any potential flying steel that might sneak out of the shaper collar and turned on the machine, the spindle turning at 2,000 rpm's. That shaper started hopping all over the floor like a Jane Fonda workout tape on fast-forward. Boy that almost scared breakfast out of me, and it was a lesson I will never forget: Make sure you weigh the knives and that they have pretty much identical weight. Mine did not weigh the same.

I weighed the knives on my balance-beam scale, and after comparing their weight, I ground away the back to make the weight very close.

Trial and error was how I was learning my craft. Except for working in a couple of shops, including Uncle Doug's, I was self-taught. But I was good with my hands, curious and patient, so my work kept getting better. Nobody—except perhaps Uncle Doug—was more surprised than I was.

My partners, Steve and Marvin, were commercial contractors and friends with a lot of movers and shakers. They used my little company to finish their projects, far beyond the reach we had on our own. "This is going to be the most significant project you'll ever do," Marvin said when we got the contract for the finishing work at Duke Zeibert's restaurant, on the southwest corner of Connecticut Avenue and L Street.

Duke Zeibert's was a destination. For decades the famous and elite dined at Duke's, which had a hierarchy on where you were seated. If you were Edward Bennett Williams, you'd be in the first few tables, Jack Kent Cooke, same place. Me, over in "Siberia," the south end of the restaurant. But it was fun just to go and see who was there.

Duke Zeibert's was an exciting project that included architectural woodwork, fabric wall panels, onyx-topped bar, mahogany-encased monolithic server stations and mahogany veneer wall panels.

"Hey kid," the larger-than-life Zeibert called out to me as I worked. "Come over and sit down a minute. How old are you anyway?" he wanted to know.

"I'm 32," I replied.

"Shit, I got neckties older than that," he retorted.

Duke's original restaurant was torn down to make way for a large office building and later reopened in 1983 on the second floor overlooking Connecticut Avenue.

The whole experience was amazing as I look back on it. I met so many Washington, D.C. legends and large personalities during that time. When the Washington Redskins won the Superbowl, we were asked to build the display case for the trophy. Later, we built a second for another trophy. Both trophy cases were just inside Zeibert's front door to the left.

ON MY OWN AGAIN
ENTERPRISE WOODCRAFT
& DESIGN COMPANY

After about four and a half years in partnership with Steve and Marvin, I joined the local chapter of the Architectural Woodwork Institute. At their chapter meetings, I met a lot of my competitors. "Sure, come on by," they'd said when I asked to visit their shops.

It was exciting and educational, learning how the shops were laid out, what equipment other shops had and why they had chosen certain machines. Some of them were already getting into the revolutionary era of computer-controlled equipment.

"I saw this amazing two-bladed table saw at Mark's shop down the street," I told Steve, "and I think it would really make things a lot easier for us."

"How much does it cost?" Steve asked.

"About $10,000," I replied.

"Are you crazy?" Steve exclaimed. "You have a new Powermatic saw. Isn't that good enough?"

Granted the $10,000 Altendorf saw was three times more expensive than the Powermatic, but I knew it would be worth it. That saw was the start of my partners' having visions of the future different from mine.

Steve and Marvin wanted to move their offices and woodworking shop out of our Quonset hut to a building they had built with some other partners. It was a public storage facility on one floor, with offices and shop space above, fronting Kenilworth Avenue. The location was sloped away from the road frontage so access to each level was at ground level.

"Marvin and I have joined a partnership in a building in Hyattsville and have decided to move the offices and woodworking shop there," Steve told me.

Wow! I was a bit shocked but probably not totally surprised.

"I think I'll stay," I said.

"What?" Steve said in an elevated voice. "How are you going to do that?" he protested.

"I guess I'll have to find another space nearby," I said, for Steve and Marvin held the lease and they were unlikely to transfer it to me.

"Who's going to finance that? Who's your new partner?" Marvin said.

"Just me," I replied.

"That's impossible, you have to have a new partner. Who is it?" Marvin almost shouted. Boy, they were not happy, for the way this was playing out was apparently not the way they thought it would go.

I sought legal advice and quickly realized that Steve and Marvin held all the cards. There were no significant assets, and I would spend more on legal fees than I would recover, a sober reality. My long-time friend Kip Tweedy had joined my company, but he wouldn't go with me. He said he needed the security of working for an established business; he was a single parent raising a daughter. I was disappointed but understood.

I walked out the door with nothing but my personal hand tools. All of the equipment we had accumulated over these many years—my beloved Powermatic Shaper, my Powermatic table saw, my joiner, planner and a ton of routers, sanders, drills—stayed with the partnership.

1986

Onward and upward.

I approached my father, who had just retired from his law practice, to ask if he would be interested in starting a new shop. He enthusiastically said *yes!*

I must admit, in hindsight, how incredible that was. He was 75, and we didn't really get along. I had problems with authority, and, as I had left school, he worried what was going to become of me.

But what was he going to do now that he had retired? He had no job, and he'd aged out of tennis. Working together turned out to be a win-win situation. Dad got a new lease on life. I got the cash I needed, and, his former law partners said, "the best partner I could ever hope for." He could keep an eye on me and, as he slipped into dementia, I on him. It was the best three or four years we ever had together. Eventually, he told me he was proud of me.

We found a small space down the street near the Walter Reed Annex, which had its own fascinating history, I learned in my spare time. The campus began in 1887 as Ye Forest Inne, a summer vacation retreat for Washington, D.C., residents. The retreat did not succeed financially, and the property was sold and redeveloped as a finishing school, opening in 1894 with a class of 48 female students. It failed in incarnation after incarnation over the years, but eventually became a rehabilitation and convalescent center for Walter Reed Army Hospital.

The architecture of the campus remained eclectic and whimsical. In addition to various Victorian styles, exotic designs included a Dutch windmill, a Swiss chalet, a Japanese pagoda, an Italian villa and an English castle. Many of these small homes with international designs were built from blueprints obtained by competing sororities, but all were designed by architect Emily Elizabeth Holman of Philadelphia,

Pennsylvania. The campus also featured covered walkways, outdoor sculptures and elaborately planned formal gardens.

Eventually the Army lost sufficient funding from the U.S. Congress to maintain the space and was compelled to declare the property excess, pending transfer to the General Services Administration to find a new owner. In 1972 the most historic part of the complex gained listing on the National Register of Historic Places as the National Park Seminary Historic District. In the new century, it became an eclectic community combining historic and new housing.

We set up our new shop space of approximately 2,500 square feet in a not-so-historic warehouse that housed our new landlord, an interior painting contractor that primarily worked on rental apartment complexes.

As before, we were faced with signing new work as well as setting up the shop with new equipment. Much of the setup included constructing a small office space in the front along with the electrical requirements of new machinery, workspace assembly areas, compressed airlines, new lighting and remediating the abundance of resin deposited on the floor by its past tenant, a cultured-resin vanity-top company. We had to use a floor sander to smooth it out.

Bill, my father, took his new partnership as a full-time job. Until he was no longer able, he'd be at his desk every day, keeping the books, doing payroll and taxes, letting me know when we were running out of money and answering the phone. Early on he would answer, "Hello."

I said, "Dad, you have to say the name of the company when you answer the phone—you know, Hello, Enterprise Woodcraft & Design."

"Oh yea, right, sorry," Dad said, in the amazing role reversal of traveling in lockstep with his son.

This new space was a new start in many ways. Initially it was just my father, me and my second wife, Patricia, a fashion consultant whose good eye helped us set up. Jim Matheson, a slender man with light brown hair, answered an early want ad. Jim turned out to be the most amazing woodworker I had ever met. His hiring was one of what became numerous serendipitous events over many years to come.

Jim, like most of us, had some quirks. He had constructed a large box that turned out to be a mouse-breeding operation.

"Really, Jim? You are raising mice?" I said. "Don't

we have enough mice loose in the warehouse that we need a display case of them?"

"I think they are cute," he said. "I kind of like them."

This became an early study of business management. I could tell Jim to get rid of the mice brothel and risk his leaving. Or I could do nothing and fume about the situation. At that time Jim was a very valuable asset, so I chose the latter strategy, for a while. He quit not long after I made him get rid of his mice.

Back in the mid-1980s, it was possible to build a portfolio of project photos and knock on doors. You could actually walk into a design firm office and ask to meet with one of the principals. The success of this strategy enabled us to start working with a number of really great design firms.

I was very fortunate to have already met and started working with Teresita and Carlos Deupi of Deupi and Associates. They were one of the top interior architecture and design firms in the D.C. market and a perfect client for a small woodworking firm. I had some competition. Another firm, A&K Woodworking, was very much entrenched at Deupi, having worked with them for many years. Alfred and Kirk, hence A&K, were first generation Americans with old-world European knowledge and skills. Their work was impeccable, and they were a formidable competitor.

Being the new kid on the Deupi block was a very lucky break for a young guy starting out.

I can't remember the first project that we did with Deupi, but I do remember that we fabricated, finished and delivered many unique reception desks for many corporate interior projects. I remember one reception desk that had some issues. It was a large desk that was approximately 20 feet long and had a triple bullnose edge on the top. The bullnose was three-quarter radius pieces about 4 inches high stacked on top of each other in projection, finished in a light blue with a high-gloss mirror finish. It was stunning.

The problem was that during installation the high-gloss bull nose had been damaged. We had to work after hours to sand and prep the damaged area, then apply the color coat and clear coat using an automotive spray product. After allowing enough time to dry, we then buffed the repaired area to blend with the rest. It worked, but we had to contend with spraying toxic chemicals in a finished commercial space along with containing the splatter of buffing compound during the repair. Our solutions were low tech, but they worked. We brought in a box fan and held up cardboard panels to catch the escaping spray. I learned that in managing our challenges we were also helping manage our clients' challenges, and going to extremes to make that happen was paramount in preserving the relationship.

Another memorable project was the Holiday Inn in Bethesda, Maryland. The parameters were a bit different and exciting. The hotel had a large circular stair in the main lobby ascending to the second floor. The mission was to clad the 24-foot high, cylindrical central column of the stairs in wood veneer panels. Sounds simple enough, right?

The catch was we had eight weeks to fabricate, finish and install the project before the end of the year or the money would run out. With the incentive of making the date or losing the fee, we worked very hard on this project, long hours, dealing with the further complication of internal production glitches. We had put quite a premium on the project and came out a winner.

A unique U-shaped conference table unleashed a lengthy relationship with Peter Hapstak, an architect; Brent Nelson, another architect who would become our main contact with Apple; and a few other memorable individuals.

The table started out as an interesting design, a splayed U-shape, 14-foot wood-top table with solid oak edges and angled steel legs. The concept was to allow everyone seated to have an uninterrupted sight line to a very large wall display. The modesty panel, attached to the legs, was perforated metal framed with aluminum angle.

We had morphed into incorporating light metal work into some of our projects. It seemed to provide an opportunity and challenge all at once. We noticed a problem after the table was assembled in the shop. You could stand at one open end of the table and push down, and the opposite end would pop up. This was not good.

"Hey Peter, we got a problem with the table and I want you to come out and see it," I told Hapstak over the phone.

"Sure," he said. "I can come out tomorrow."

Before Peter arrived, we did some analysis and came up with a couple of fixes.

Peter looked at the table and said, "Wow, that's not going to work."

We talked for a while and all agreed that if we added a gusset to every table leg at the floor, it would counteract the undulation.

The U-shaped table was a success. We built several, and most were incorporated into the rest of the many executive briefing center projects Apple built in major cities around the country.

My gamble had worked. My white-collar father had turned into my main supporter, working with me every step of the way, even sharing the load of raising walls and hanging drywall. With a handful of new woodworkers under my continuing self-taught education, Enterprise Woodcraft & Design was playing with the big boys, with clients like Apple.

After a few years in the first location, we decided to move to a larger space, always a risk: more overhead, more people, more equipment.

1989

Monard Drive in Silver Spring was a warehouse development with numerous buildings. We decided on a space about 8,500 square feet. This space had one loading dock door next to a large metal entry door, not ideal, but workable.

Peter Hapstak, the architect, did the office layout and we did a plant layout, taking a large scale drawing of the space and making little cutouts that represented the equipment. Moving the little cutouts around was an efficient way to see relationships of equipment, necessary feed- and run-out space for parts and product to move through and around the space.

Hapstak's design was unique and thought through. Everything had to be built to code, which for a woodworking shop entails some extra expenses, mostly electrical, dust collection and a 24-inch diameter hole fitted with a pipe that ran through the finishing booth roof for the exhaust.

The decade or so we worked on Monard Drive was possibly our most productive and successful time. Many of the projects won awards and were published in national design magazines. We even were awarded a few American Institute of Architects awards.

I wasn't shy about taking on challenging, some would say crazy, projects. I suppose it was a personal need for risk and challenge because pushing the envelope edge was not necessarily the best business decision. Too many projects did not make any money, which is the currency of survival.

One project, a telecommunications company retail store, morphed into three. Part of the design was an elliptical sales counter topped by an elliptical perforated panel for signage and lighting. To construct the lighting and signage component, we had to figure out how to bend steel. I was fascinated, for the best part of any project is figuring out how to make it a reality.

Steel can be bent. You actually roll-form the material, in this case a 7-gauge 3-by-6-inch structural steel tube. The tubing is filled with rosin, machine-formed in rollers, then heated to remove the rosin. The rosin prevents the tube from collapsing during the rolling process.

I had found a guy in Baltimore who did this type of work. When we spoke and I told him what we needed done, he said, "You want that rolled the hard way or the easy way?"

"I don't understand," I said.

"I can roll the elliptical shape with the 6-inch leg vertical, the easy way, or I can roll the tube with the 3-inch leg vertical, the hard way."

"We want the hard way," I said, for we needed the 6-inch leg horizontal.

The list of projects we made during that decade—both money-making and not—contains many, many unique, challenging and beautiful spaces—so many I have not dared to count them.

THE WALTER EPISODE

He cautiously walked into the plant, possibly curious about the noise or the open loading dock door. Almost completely black, he had white accents on his face and paws. Initially I thought, man, you are in the wrong place, but every time I would put him outside, he would sneak back in. I was perplexed. I was not a cat person by definition and was not thinking of converting. This stranger had no collar or identifying info, and these were the days before many pets were chipped. I asked around the warehouse complex to see who he belonged to, but no one said he was theirs. A friend said it was not uncommon for young cats to wander off and forget where they had started from, kinda like a walkabout.

It sure seemed like I was stuck with him.

Walter seemed like a good name for cat who was strong, inquisitive and independent. I took him to a vet to get him looked over while I continued the search.

The vet said he was in good shape but should probably get fixed at his young age before other complications arose. I went all in.

I moved him into the house I was renting on the South River outside Annapolis. It didn't enter my mind that bringing in a new cat would be upsetting the balance of the neighborhood. It didn't take long before I heard commotion late one evening. There was no question that Walter, who I had let wonder outside from time to time, had gotten into it with an older resident of the community. He was missing part of his left ear when he returned. It didn't look too bad, and I had no idea what to do from a medical perspective. He survived.

On a later evening, the commotion was much more intense, and I found him outside the door with his belly slit open. The vet said she couldn't suture this type of wound. I would need to keep an eye on him and periodically apply antibiotics, letting it heal from the inside. Walter was not a fan. At one point I decided to give him a bath. He reluctantly complied only because I had him by the back of his neck. He was clearly embarrassed in his matted fur post-bath wet state. We called a truce.

1996

During our time at Monard Drive, we added new, computer-driven technologies that enabled us to be more productive—once we figured out how to use them. One was known then as a point-to-point machine, basically a computer-numeric-controlled machine, CNC, with routing and drilling capability. With these machines you had to write what is called G-Code to tell the different operations what to do and where to do it. The codes for the X to Y coordinates move the drill or router bit in and out and right to left. The Z coordinate is used for up and down for depth.

Not just anyone can write the G-code, we soon found. By serendipity, we had Dave, who knew how to write code. It took ages, but we made it work for a year or so until I discovered drafting software combined with a post-processor software that would translate the code to the actual machine.

In making base cabinets, this machine would notch the toe kick, add a groove on one side for the cabinet back panel, drill holes for all the assembly dowels and drill different-size holes for shelf-support hardware. All this would cycle in a few minutes. Better still, the machine was split so that you could machine one part and load the next at the same time, then switch sides. The point-to-point machine made us very productive, and we took on more work, cabinet and case work that could be machine controlled rather than hand made.

But craftsmanship was still our biggest distinction. The artisanal quality of our work brought us possibly the most prestigious project we ever did, the Federal Reserve Boardroom renovation.

The Federal Reserve, the United States central banking system and thus a global economic regulator, dates back to 1913, and its offices on Pennsylvania Avenue reflect that historic character. The original map of the United States with its 12 Federal Reserve regions, some 24 feet square, hung on the east wall.

A half dozen different trades, electricians to wood workers, contributed their skills to the renovation of the Boardroom from the walls out, including the installation of newer audio-and-visual technology upgrades, which needed to be disguised into door capitals to hide the upgrade. As the room's centerpiece, Enterprise Woodcraft and Design fabricated, finished and installed a 27-foot-long mahogany table with a granite center inlay. The table carried a bunch of technology itself: microphones, speakers and a control drawer at the chairman's seat to operate the lighting, drop down AV screens, window coverings and projectors. It was all choreographed like a ballet. For many years my son would call me every time the table was on the news: "Hey Dad, your table is on the news again."

The work started as a night job. I hate night jobs. They're like going to work when you normally sit down for dinner, really messing up your rhythm. We worked not only night but also on a tentative schedule. Should the Fed Board need to meet, our work would be suspended at a moment's notice. Then the entire area would be electronically swept for listening devices. That happened only once. Once was enough to convince the decision makers that mobilizing, then shutting down such a workforce was unsustainable. With that decision, we were switched to a regular day schedule.

At the completion of the project, Chairman Alan Greenspan addressed us all in a large thank-you moment.

In 1985, I had married a second time. Patricia Shaker was a beautiful woman and quite a combo of her

Lebanese father and Italian mother. She had studied as a concert pianist at the Cincinnati Conservatory, and when I met her at Georgetown Park, then a high-end mall in its glory years, was working in high-end retail.

Eventually, Patricia joined me at the plant, handling the money, receivables, payables and yes, payroll and taxes.

Riding high as we were, I thought we were making money. I was wrong.

"I have made a huge mistake," Patricia told me back when I thought nothing could go wrong. I expected her to say she'd had an affair. Her confession was much worse.

"I have not made any federal tax withholding payments all year," she said.

"What?" I exclaimed, "You're kidding, right?"

She was not. She'd skipped the payments, she said, to protect me from knowing we were losing, not making, money. She thought me so distracted and emotionally fragile as a result of recent traumatic events in my family that I could not bear the truth. Month after month, it became harder and harder to confess.

"I think we owe you guys some money," I had to admit to the IRS.

"Yep, you do."

Fail to file your payroll withholding taxes, and the IRS charges penalty and interest, usually totaling around 18 percent. In addition, the Payroll Recovery Act automatically doubles the amount of the taxes you owe.

In our case, the debt was six figures. We entered into a payment plan and were successful enough to pay off the IRS in less than three years.

Patricia and I went our separate ways, and my elder son Jason, then 26, took over payroll.

1999

Squared with the IRS, we were able to move from being renters to owners. 4000 Pennwood Road was an immense 15,000 square foot warehouse just outside D.C. in Prince Georges County. Previously home to a large printing company, the space had some pluses, central air conditioning being one of them. But the immense AC unit consumed natural gas like an athlete drinking Gatorade so we didn't run it much. I'd grown my business from the original two to three to, at peak, 23, and just about everyone came with me when we moved to the new plant.

My sister, who had lent me part of the purchase price, then joined the business, bringing us real financial skills.

Our fourth location needed the usual work: compressed airlines, dust collection ductwork, electric for large and small equipment, ventilation holes in the roof and more. We moved in with the help of the rigging company who moved the massive multi-ton equipment we had accumulated over the years.

Bill Norlin—author, entrepreneur, woodworker— helped with plant and equipment layout. Bill was the originator of the MMP degree. He explained that specialized degree in this way: "I go into a lot of plants, meet a bunch of people and many ask whether I have an MBA, engineering degree or architectural degree. I tell them I have an MMP degree. It means Made Many Payrolls, and I think it expresses great value and its own unique classification. For folks like myself who have worked on both sides of the office door, processing and funding payrolls is a significant accomplishment."

I have used the designation ever since.

With a drive-in garage door at one end, twin loading dock doors at the other and our finishing department somewhere in the middle, the new space functioned very well. We did a number of law firm projects, most including high-end finishes with a conference table, wood veneer wall panels and a reception desk.

Boise Schiller Flexner LLP was one such firm. For them, we constructed a conference room from reclaimed barn beams complete with exposed notches and peg holes. The beams were set at a 10-degree angle inward and connected with veneer panels perforated for sound. The sandwich of veneer panels between the beams, to contain acoustic material for sound deadening, worked quite well.

Squire Sanders was another law firm for whom we did multiple projects. From their D.C. enclave on Pennsylvania Avenue to their Brussels, Belgium, office we made furnishings, tables, secretarial stations and incorporated metal assemblies.

Brussels was an interesting install. The award-winning architect designer Philip Olson and I were the installation team. The whole process, building and finishing the product, crating everything and shipping to Belgium was full of great lessons and experiences—notwithstanding the fact that were Phil and I were the only two people on site who spoke English. Our work took longer than Phil expected, but we were comforted by way too many visits to Rick's Café Americain.

Back home, my company and I worked through the usual adversity, with managing people the toughest part of the job. One of those squabbles set Elaine Wilson from our finishing department, against our fine furniture finisher Art Weinman. Art, she said, had told her that this was a man's company.

I felt a chill go up my spine as I contemplated a law suit from one of the crew.

I confronted Art. "Did you tell Elaine this was a man's company?" I asked him.

Art stiffened and took a step back. "Randy, I have reached my limit," he told me. "Elaine's constant harassment and sexual references are more that I can put up with."

I was in momentary shock. All sorts of thoughts were going through my head, and it started to hurt. "What are your telling me?"

"Just kidding," Art said.

Boy that was an adrenalin surge. To my relief, the dispute wore itself out.

One of the workers who made the move with me was Scott, a determined young man who seemed to rise above adversity. He rode his bike to work, for after too many DUI's he no longer had a valid drivers license. A lanky guy with blond hair, he occasionally would get into a tirade about his work in the panel-layup area. Yet he would do the work of two people. You just had to endure the shouts and bumping noise. Nothing suffered ill effects. It was just Scott.

Scott was married and had a small child, but he was living with his mother. Still, I was surprised the day he told me his mother had asked him to talk with me.

"Sure, Scott. What's up?"

"I want to start expressing my feminine side at work," he said.

"OK, Scott, what does that mean?" I asked, thinking *what is going on here?*

"Tomorrow, I'm going to be wearing a pair of hot pants along with a padded bra and will have my hair in a pony tail," he announced. "My mother said I should alert you before I came in."

Don't react, don't react was swimming through my head.

"I wanted to see if you think it will be disruptive to the guys in the shop," Scott said.

"Actually I think you are good, Scott. I think everybody thinks you are already a bit weird, so they won't notice," I said.

The next day Scott did not disappoint, and everyone took it in stride with a long glance and a head shake.

2001

Someplace along the way, my focus changed from making the best product we could to making money.

That switch changed the culture of the company. It was in many ways the beginning of the end.

Too many financially unsuccessful projects over the course of a couple years had drained our cash to the point that we were struggling month to month. The final nail came on the project for EDS, Ross Perot's old company. A dreaded night job, it was doomed from the beginning. It seemed everything that could, did go wrong. We struggled at the end and, though we finished the project, no one was very happy—including me.

Starting and building a company is hard work, believe me, but shrinking a company can be even harder. The shrinking part can eventually lead to just giving up.

It was just after 911. We had watched the planes fly into the Trade Center buildings. Altogether, the combined stress and emotional pressure became unbearable.

By the end of October, I had decided to shut down the company and finish the few projects we had.

I put everything up for sale. The buyers came, all of my competitors, for most of the smaller equipment and a few larger pieces. The large Computer Numeric Control machine, case clamp and digital Altendorf table saw (boy I still miss that saw!) I sold to another shop in Virginia. I held the note and took payments.

I knew this was a form of embezzlement, for I had signed a deal with GE Capital when the building was purchased and rolled the larger equipment into the almost seven-figure deal. Before long, I got the guilts.

"I'm embezzling from you," I told my loan officer in a confessional phone call. "I sold some of the equipment and am taking payments."

"What are you doing with the money?" GE Capital wanted to know.

"I am making loan payments to you," I said.

During a few minutes on hold, I thought this was the end of everything. I was pleasantly surprised, finally, to learn that as long as the loan was performing, GE was good.

I rented out part of the building and lived in the other part. Industrial as it was, it was one of the best times of my life. Parking my car in the living room seemed to be entirely appropriate.

My renter turned out to be an ex-D.C. police officer who operated a black, gay strip club in my building. That was a learning curve, on so many levels. After seven months of no rent payments, I was able to finally evict the tenant. It took three attempts and testimony in landlord-tenant court, but I was persistent.

After shutting down the company at 49 years old, I went to work for the Architectural Woodwork Institute. I was able to hold on to the building until 2006, when it sold with a substantial profit.

Nowadays, I do some reflecting on what I achieved in 21 years. In 1980 I was 28 years old, and after the expulsion by Uncle Doug I was all of a sudden in business. I suppose I could have gotten a job with another company, but I was much too stubborn for that. Proving everyone wrong had been my motivation for some time.

Thus motivated, I grew a company from nothing to a multi-million dollar corporation, I tell myself. I purchased our own warehouse, which turned out to be my shrewdest move, for I earned more money in real estate than I ever did in woodwork. For our customers, we went above and beyond, doing fine work in wood and more, meeting every deadline, and never letting them see us sweat.

The company I built helped 23 people support their families. Before I closed down, I made sure everyone of them had a job.

So, yeah, I tell myself. It was time well spent.

ACKNOWLEDGMENTS

I would like to thank the following folks for their support in writing this assemblage:

My wife Marie Bundy, whose unwavering support helped get me here.

Carol Durrough and Laurie Buell for being my sisters and filling in my memory.

My good friends John Little and Pat Griffin for their honest feedback.

Martha Gould, friend of my youth, who was there in the Bomber story.

Mary Blayney, whose early encouragement kept me going.

Bob Whitsell, who told me I could write.

Editor Sandra Olivetti Martin, who said that missing college writing courses is probably the reason I can write.

Troy Juliar and Bob Berberich as first readers.

Anne Arundel County Library assistant Connie Trent for finding articles on the Bomber.

Suzanne Shelden for making this look pretty good!

ABOUT THE AUTHOR

Randy Estabrook was born in Washington, D.C., and grew up in Bethesda, Maryland. His father was an accomplished intellectual property attorney and his mother a talented oil painter Randy's first job after leaving high school early was at Empire Music record store. He founded and operated his woodworking company for 20 years and later joined the staff of the Architectural Woodwork Institute as program director and later executive director of the Quality Certification Program. Randy continues to do small woodwork projects such as his recently completed live-edge walnut dining table. He and his wife Marie Bundy live in Calvert County, Maryland, on the shores of the Chesapeake Bay and are active ceramic artists, boaters and community activists.